ULTIMATE

MOM EXPERIENCE COUPONS

SON EDITION

A Keepsake Journal of

Mother – Son Memories

Joy Holiday Family

We do not remember days, we remember moments.

Cesare Pavese

Copyright © 2021 by Joy Holiday Publishing
All rights reserved. No part of this book may be reproduced or used in any manner without written permission of the copyright owner except for the use of quotations in a book review.

Book Design by Joy Holiday Publishing LLC

ISBN 978-1-956146-06-6

Images used under license from Canva.com

Capture the MOMENTS
while you make the MEMORIES

You know your mom is special, so get her the perfect gift! This book is the ultimate in mother-son coupon gift-giving with 52 thoughtful and entertaining coupons for sons to give their moms. That's enough coupons to have one for every week of the entire calendar year.

This keepsake journal is meant to chronicle not just the gift giving but the actual redemptions of the coupons. This gorgeous book takes the coupon idea to the next level. Each activity is designed as an elegant ticket. The large, easy-to-read coupon tickets and redemption stubs are meant to stay in the book. Next to each coupon page is a space to place a photo and write what you did together.

There is also an additional page of smaller coupons replicating the larger tickets that may be cut out as part of the fun. This book is the solution to unused coupon books or gifts that are not part of a larger experience. Families can look back on all the special experiences they created together throughout the year.

With these coupon prompts, moms get to spend quality time with their loved ones and time doing the things that they love on their own. This book includes activities for moms of all ages. We have even included some extra blank tickets since you know your mother best. Is your mom a skydiving enthusiast, golfer, or gamer? You can fill in the blank!

We hope you'll use this book to create lots of beautiful moments together!

Joy Holiday Family

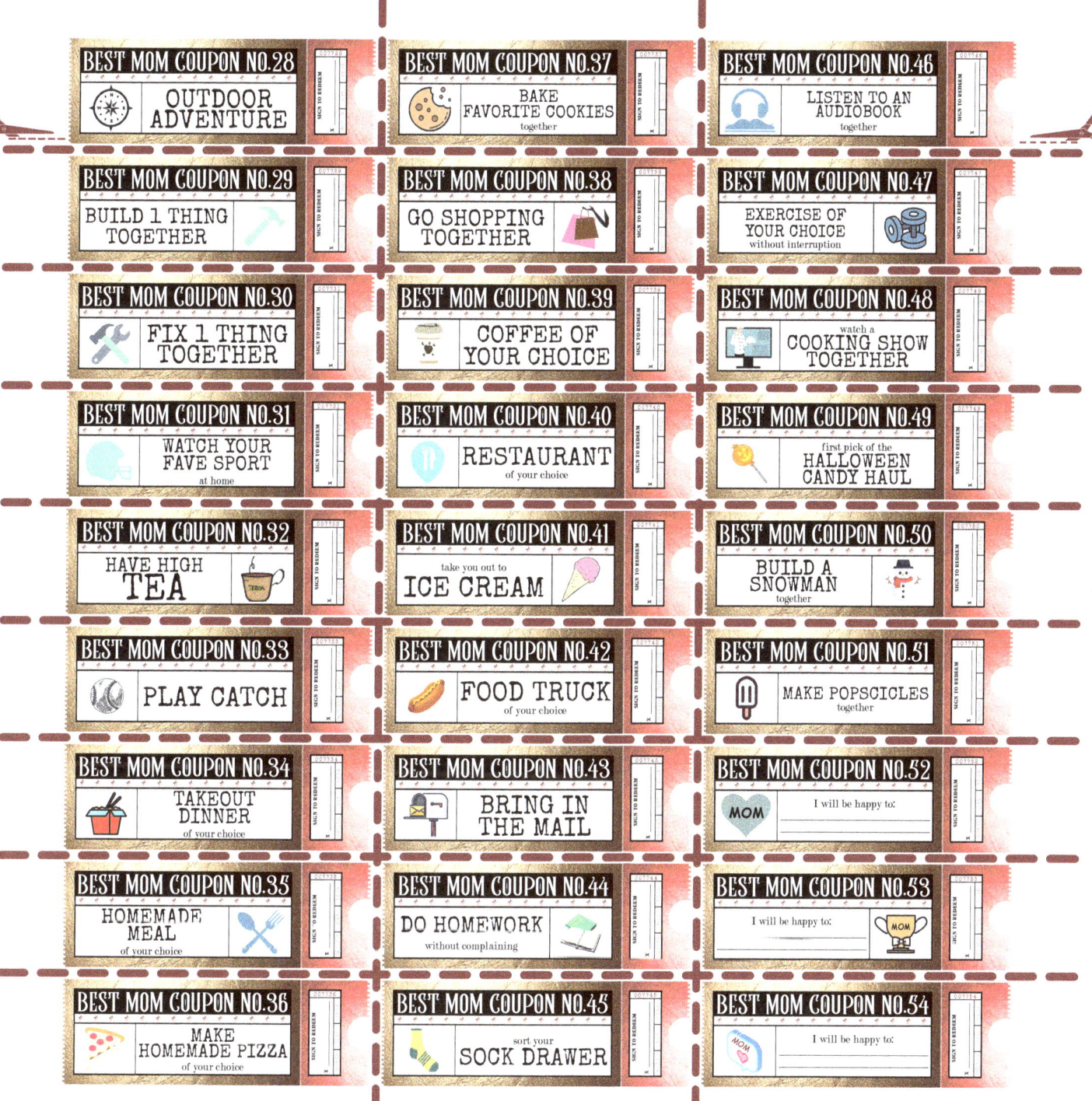

BEST MOM COUPON NO.01

 **BREAKFAST IN BED**

BEST MOM COUPON NO.02

NAP
without interruption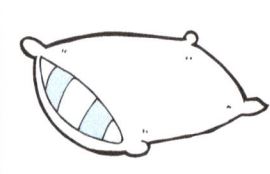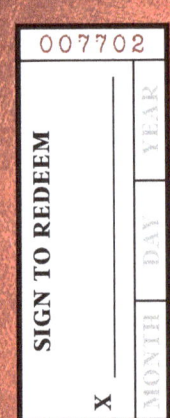

BEST MOM COUPON NO.03

 **SLEEPING IN**
undisturbed

HOW DID WE HAVE FUN?

Who

What

Where

BEST MOM COUPON NO.04

 one day without **COMPLAINING**

007704
SIGN TO REDEEM
X ___
MONTH DAY YEAR

BEST MOM COUPON NO.05

one day filled with **COMPLIMENTS**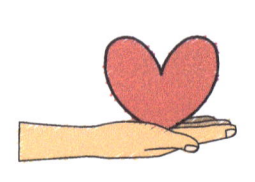

007705
SIGN TO REDEEM
X ___
MONTH DAY YEAR

BEST MOM COUPON NO.06

 **CALLING YOU "MA'AM"** all day long, or the title of your choice

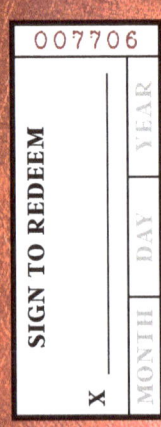
007706
SIGN TO REDEEM
X ___
MONTH DAY YEAR

HOW DID WE HAVE FUN?

Who

What

Where

BEST MOM COUPON NO.07

PERSONAL ASSISTANT
for the day

007707
SIGN TO REDEEM
X _____
MONTH | DAY | YEAR

BEST MOM COUPON NO.08

listen to & laugh at
1 MOM JOKE

007708
SIGN TO REDEEM
X _____
MONTH | DAY | YEAR

BEST MOM COUPON NO.09

attentively listen to 1 session of
MOM ADVICE

007709
SIGN TO REDEEM
X _____
MONTH | DAY | YEAR

HOW DID WE HAVE FUN?

Who

What

Where

BEST MOM COUPON NO.10

give you one gigantic
BEAR HUG

007710

SIGN TO REDEEM

X | MONTH | DAY | YEAR

BEST MOM COUPON NO.11

DANCE PARTY

007711

SIGN TO REDEEM

X | MONTH | DAY | YEAR

BEST MOM COUPON NO.12

house & car
DJ FOR THE DAY

007712

SIGN TO REDEEM

X | MONTH | DAY | YEAR

HOW DID WE HAVE FUN?

Who

What

Where

BEST MOM COUPON NO.13

CAR DETAIL
clean the inside of your ride

007713

SIGN TO REDEEM

X _____

MONTH | DAY | YEAR

BEST MOM COUPON NO.14

CAR WASH
by hand

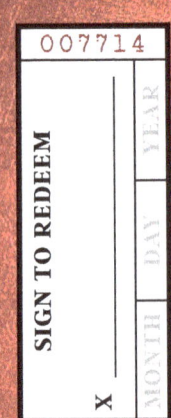

007714

SIGN TO REDEEM

X _____

MONTH | DAY | YEAR

BEST MOM COUPON NO.15

PLANT FLOWERS

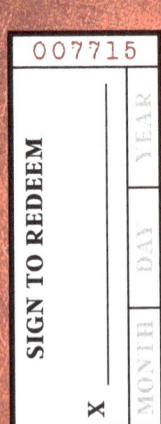

007715

SIGN TO REDEEM

X _____

MONTH | DAY | YEAR

HOW DID WE HAVE FUN?

Who

What

Where

BEST MOM COUPON NO.16

TAKE OUT THE TRASH

007716
SIGN TO REDEEM
X _____
MONTH / DAY / YEAR

BEST MOM COUPON NO.17

GO FOR A WALK
together

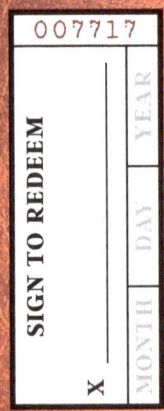
007717
SIGN TO REDEEM
X _____
MONTH / DAY / YEAR

BEST MOM COUPON NO.18

OUTDOOR CHORE
of your choice

007718
SIGN TO REDEEM
X _____
MONTH / DAY / YEAR

HOW DID WE HAVE FUN?

Who

What

Where

BEST MOM COUPON NO.19

wash, dry, & fold
YOUR LAUNDRY

007719

SIGN TO REDEEM

X _____ MONTH | DAY | YEAR

BEST MOM COUPON NO.20

CHORE
of your choice

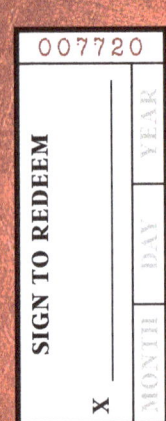

007720

SIGN TO REDEEM

X _____ MONTH | DAY | YEAR

BEST MOM COUPON NO.21

ORGANIZE
your _____

007721

SIGN TO REDEEM

X _____ MONTH | DAY | YEAR

HOW DID WE HAVE FUN?

Who

What

Where

BEST MOM COUPON NO.22

SPA DAY

007722
SIGN TO REDEEM
X _____
MONTH DAY YEAR

BEST MOM COUPON NO.23

MOVIE NIGHT
movie of your choice

007723
SIGN TO REDEEM
X _____
MONTH DAY YEAR

BEST MOM COUPON NO.24

uninterrupted GAMING

007724
SIGN TO REDEEM
X _____
MONTH DAY YEAR

HOW DID WE HAVE FUN?

Who

What

Where

BEST MOM COUPON NO.25

BOARD GAME
of your choice

007725
SIGN TO REDEEM
X____ MONTH DAY YEAR

BEST MOM COUPON NO.26

OUTDOOR GAME
of your choice

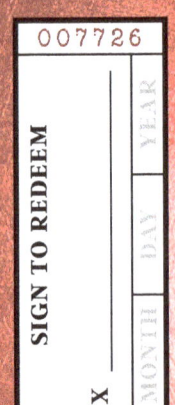
007726
SIGN TO REDEEM
X____ MONTH DAY YEAR

BEST MOM COUPON NO.27

VIDEO GAME
of your choice

007727
SIGN TO REDEEM
X____ MONTH DAY YEAR

HOW DID WE HAVE FUN?

Who

What

Where

BEST MOM COUPON NO.28

 OUTDOOR ADVENTURE

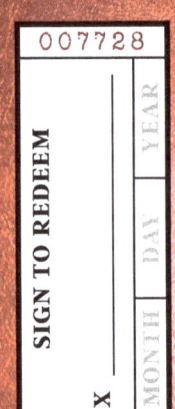
007728
SIGN TO REDEEM
X _____
MONTH | DAY | YEAR

BEST MOM COUPON NO.29

BUILD 1 THING TOGETHER

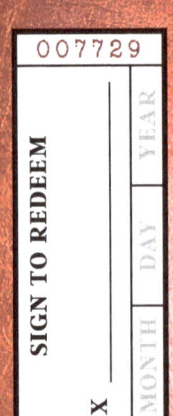
007729
SIGN TO REDEEM
X _____
MONTH | DAY | YEAR

BEST MOM COUPON NO.30

 FIX 1 THING TOGETHER

007731
SIGN TO REDEEM
X _____
MONTH | DAY | YEAR

HOW DID WE HAVE FUN?

Who

What

Where

BEST MOM COUPON NO.31

WATCH YOUR FAVE SPORT

at home

007731

SIGN TO REDEEM

X _____

MONTH | DAY | YEAR

BEST MOM COUPON NO.32

HAVE HIGH TEA

007732

SIGN TO REDEEM

X _____

MONTH | DAY | YEAR

BEST MOM COUPON NO.33

PLAY CATCH

007733

SIGN TO REDEEM

X _____

MONTH | DAY | YEAR

HOW DID WE HAVE FUN?

Who

What

Where

BEST MOM COUPON NO. 34

TAKEOUT DINNER
of your choice

007734

SIGN TO REDEEM

X _____ MONTH / DAY / YEAR

BEST MOM COUPON NO. 35

HOMEMADE MEAL
of your choice

007735

SIGN TO REDEEM

X _____ MONTH / DAY / YEAR

BEST MOM COUPON NO. 36

MAKE HOMEMADE PIZZA
of your choice

007736

SIGN TO REDEEM

X _____ MONTH / DAY / YEAR

HOW DID WE HAVE FUN?

Who

What

Where

BEST MOM COUPON NO.37

BAKE FAVORITE COOKIES
together

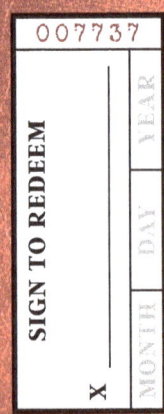

007737

SIGN TO REDEEM

X _____ MONTH / DAY / YEAR

BEST MOM COUPON NO.38

GO SHOPPING TOGETHER

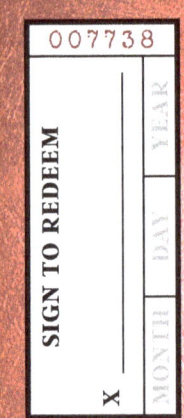

007738

SIGN TO REDEEM

X _____ MONTH / DAY / YEAR

BEST MOM COUPON NO.39

COFFEE OF YOUR CHOICE

007739

SIGN TO REDEEM

X _____ MONTH / DAY / YEAR

HOW DID WE HAVE FUN?

Who

What

Where

BEST MOM COUPON NO. 40

RESTAURANT
of your choice

007740

SIGN TO REDEEM

X _____ MONTH / DAY / YEAR

BEST MOM COUPON NO. 41

take you out to
ICE CREAM

007741

SIGN TO REDEEM

X _____ MONTH / DAY / YEAR

BEST MOM COUPON NO. 42

FOOD TRUCK
of your choice

007742

SIGN TO REDEEM

X _____ MONTH / DAY / YEAR

HOW DID WE HAVE FUN?

Who

What

Where

BEST MOM COUPON NO. 43

BRING IN THE MAIL

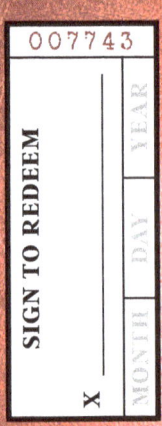

007743
SIGN TO REDEEM
X _____
MONTH / DAY / YEAR

BEST MOM COUPON NO. 44

DO HOMEWORK
without complaining

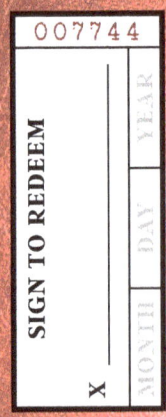

007744
SIGN TO REDEEM
X _____
MONTH / DAY / YEAR

BEST MOM COUPON NO. 45

sort your
SOCK DRAWER

007745
SIGN TO REDEEM
X _____
MONTH / DAY / YEAR

HOW DID WE HAVE FUN?

Who

What

Where

BEST MOM COUPON NO. 46

LISTEN TO AN AUDIOBOOK
together

007746
SIGN TO REDEEM
MONTH / DAY / YEAR

BEST MOM COUPON NO. 47

EXERCISE OF YOUR CHOICE
without interruption

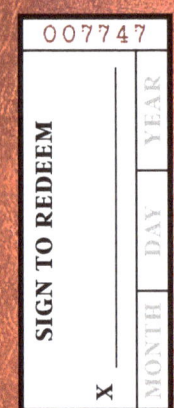
007747
SIGN TO REDEEM
MONTH / DAY / YEAR

BEST MOM COUPON NO. 48

watch a
COOKING SHOW TOGETHER

007748
SIGN TO REDEEM
MONTH / DAY / YEAR

HOW DID WE HAVE FUN?

Who

What

Where

BEST MOM COUPON NO.49

first pick of the
HALLOWEEN CANDY HAUL

007749

SIGN TO REDEEM

X ___ MONTH DAY YEAR

BEST MOM COUPON NO.50

BUILD A SNOWMAN
together

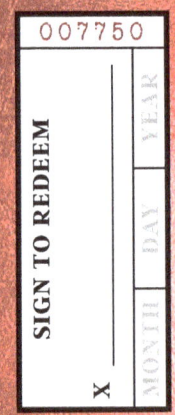

007750

SIGN TO REDEEM

X ___ MONTH DAY YEAR

BEST MOM COUPON NO.51

MAKE POPSCICLES
together

007751

SIGN TO REDEEM

X ___ MONTH DAY YEAR

HOW DID WE HAVE FUN?

Who

What

Where

BEST MOM COUPON NO.52

I will be happy to:
_____
_____

007752
SIGN TO REDEEM
X _____
MONTH DAY YEAR

BEST MOM COUPON NO.53

I will be happy to:
_____
_____

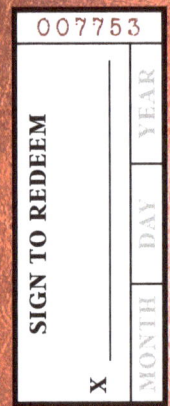

007753
SIGN TO REDEEM
X _____
MONTH DAY YEAR

BEST MOM COUPON NO.54

I will be happy to:
_____
_____

007754
SIGN TO REDEEM
X _____
MONTH DAY YEAR

HOW DID WE HAVE FUN?

Who

What

Where